Henry's Big Kaboom

A Children's Sing-along Ballad

Written and illustrated by

Mary Ames Mitchell

PeachPlumPress

www.PeachPlumPress.com

Text set in Adobe Caslon Pro.
Illustrations created using Adobe Illustrator.
Text line-edited by Jane Merryman.

Library of Congress Control Number: 2017949338

ISBN for print paperback: 978-0-9850530-9-3
ISBN for print hardback: 978-0-9991505-0-4

Summary: During the early days of the American Revolution, Colonel Henry Knox fetches the cannon and other big guns from the recently captured Fort Ticonderoga and Crown Point. With the help of patriotic countrymen, he transports the fifty-eight tons of artillery over the lakes and through the forests of Massachusetts to Cambridge, then Dorchester Heights overlooking Boston.

This ballad can be sung to the folk tune "Turkey in the Straw." You can watch and listen to sing-along animated versions of this book on YouTube through links on the website www.henrysbigkaboom.com.

Chords for the verses: G

Grandpa's name was Henry Knox
and he worked for Washington.
He joined the Revolution
D⁷
and the British took his home.

Henry's home had been in Boston,
but the Red Coats chased him out.
So, he and his fellow countrymen
decided to fight back.

All the Patriots formed an army.
North and South would work together.
They were called the Continentals.
They would fight in any weather.

But an army is no army
if there's no artillery.
"I know where we can find some guns.
I'll fetch them," said Henry.

Meanwhile in Cambridge,

Chords for the chorus: G
George Washington waited,
soldiers were baited,
C
ready to chase the British away.

'Cause what did Henry plan to do?
Blast those mighty cannon
with a big kaboom!

Henry knew some guns were left behind
in Fort Ticonderoga
back when Benedict and Ethan claimed
the fort some months before that.

Cambridge –
General
Washington's
Headquarters

But, the trouble was, 300 miles
lay 'tween the fort and Boston.
"That's no matter," Henry said to George.
"I'll find a way to get them."

Cambridge

Boston
Dorchester

Boston –
General Howe's
Headquarters

When his fellow soldiers said, "No way,
those guns are very heavy."
"Never fear, for we shall find a way,"
declared determined Henry.

Then the jolly man, who was quite large,
climbed up onto his horse.
When Henry set his mind to task,
he always kept his course.

George Washington waited,
soldiers were baited,
ready to chase the British away.

'Cause what did Henry plan to do?
Blast those mighty cannon
with a big kaboom!

Henry found the guns in disarray.
He counted fifty-nine.
He looked them over carefully
and said, "These will do fine."

Cannon

Cohorn

Mortar

Wooden Stock

Shot

Some were cannon in their wooden stocks,
and mortars fat and squat.
There were cohorns and small howitzers
with mounds and mounds of shot.

Howitzer

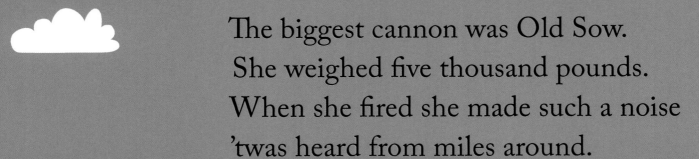

The biggest cannon was Old Sow.
She weighed five thousand pounds.
When she fired she made such a noise
'twas heard from miles around.

They placed her on the largest barge
to sail across the lake.
If she fell into the water,
it would be a big mistake.

George Washington waited,
soldiers were baited,
ready to chase the British away.

'Cause what did Henry plan to do?
Blast those mighty cannon
with a big kaboom!

Henry's men rowed through the bitter cold
to reach the other side,
where the frozen-over rivers
would allow the guns to slide.

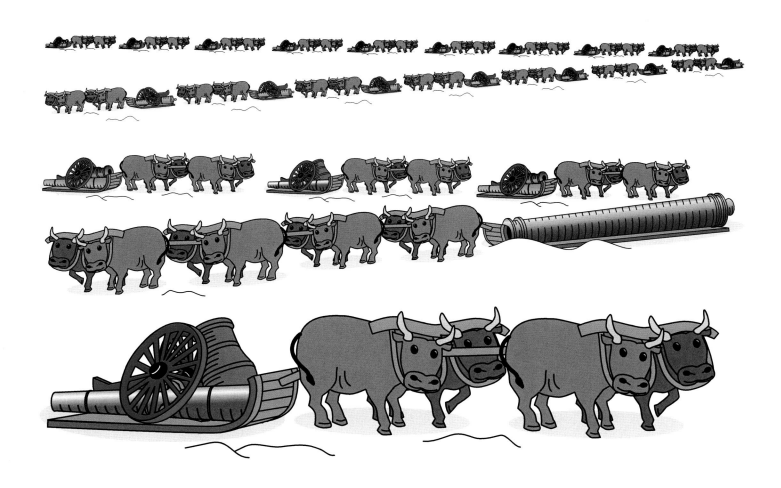

With eighty yoke of oxen,
pulling forty wooden sleds,
they could drag the big guns over ice
and through the snowy beds.

Going down one hill so steep and high,
they call it Jacob's Ladder,
the heavy guns began to slide,
going faster, faster, faster.

"Careful," Henry yelled, "Don't let them fall.
Hold on with all your might!"
That's exactly what his teamsters did,
they held the guns real tight.

People came from all around about
to aid with heavy labor –
from the nearby towns and local farms,
each out to help his neighbor.

Through the deep dark forests and
the muddy swamps, they pulled those rigs.
It was quite a task, but they held fast
and forged their way toward Cambridge,

where

George Washington waited,
soldiers were baited,
ready to chase the British away.

'Cause what did Henry plan to do?'
Blast those mighty cannon
with a big kaboom!

In the month of March, they finally reached
their hoped-for destination,
where two thousand men were needed
to prepare the guns for action.

Four hundred oxen pulled them to
the top of Dorchester Heights,
where on Boston Town those guns looked down.
It was a frightening sight.

Gabion
(Basket of Dirt and Rocks)

When the Brits woke up the following morn,
huge muzzles faced toward them.
"Oh no!" they cried, "we're going to die!
We must get out of Boston."

Fascines
(Bundled Sticks)

Chandelier
(Wooden Frame)

They turned to General William Howe,
who answered with a grunt,
"Those rebels have done more this night,
than my men in a month."

Howe said to his men,
"Quick, board your ships and sail to Halifax."
Henry's guns had done their job without
a single cannon blast.

The Patriots could return once more
to their homes back in Boston.
The guns would fight another day.
A long war lay before them.

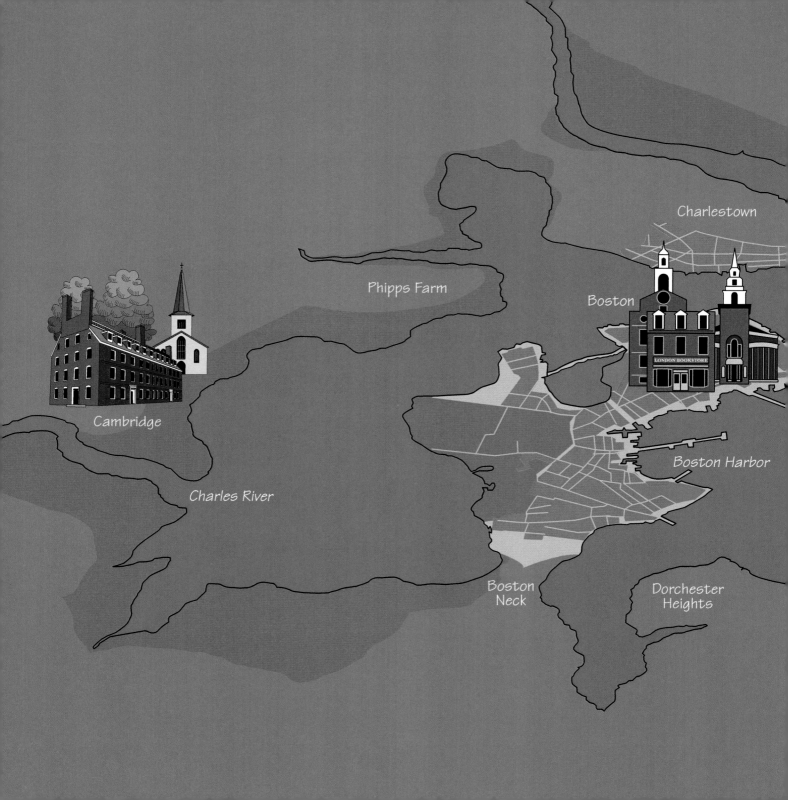

Charlestown

Boston

LONDON BOOKSTORE

Phipps Farm

Cambridge

Charles River

Boston Harbor

Boston
Neck

Dorchester
Heights

George Washington waited,
soldiers were baited,
ready to chase the British away.
'Cause what did Henry plan to do?

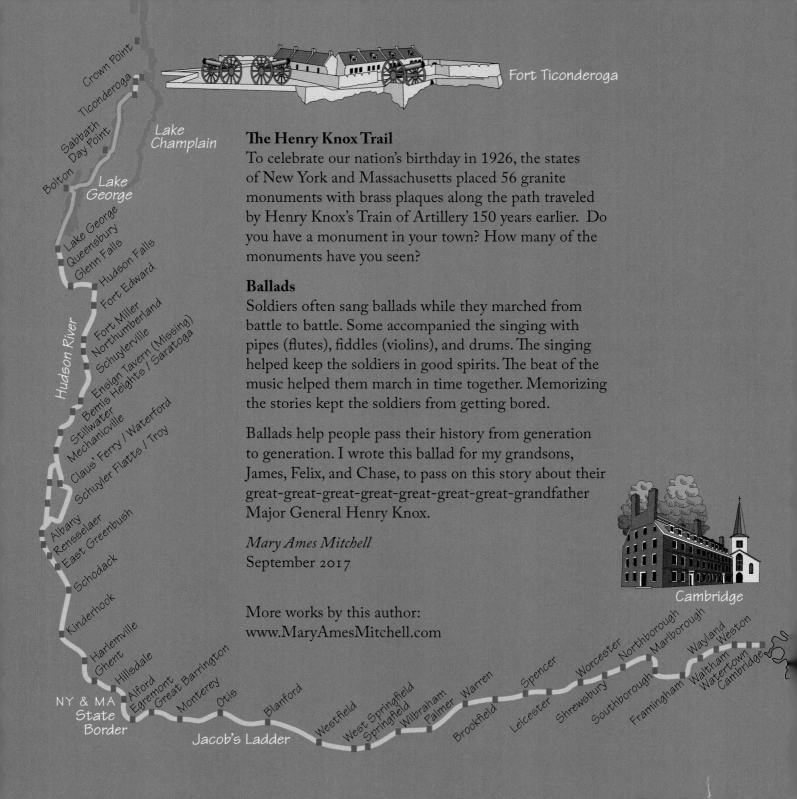

Fort Ticonderoga

Crown Point
Ticonderoga
Sabbath Day Point
Lake Champlain
Bolton
Lake George
Lake George
Queensbury
Glenn Falls
Hudson Falls
Fort Edward
Fort Miller
Northumberland
Schuylerville
Ensign Tavern (Missing)
Bemis Heights / Saratoga
Stillwater
Mechanicville
Claus' Ferry / Waterford
Schuyler Flatts / Troy
Hudson River
Albany
Rensselaer
East Greenbush
Schodack
Kinderhook
Harlemville
Ghent
Hillsdale
Alford
Egremont
Great Barrington
Monterey
Otis
NY & MA State Border
Jacob's Ladder
Blanford
Westfield
West Springfield
Springfield
Wilbraham
Palmer
Warren
Brookfield
Leicester
Spencer
Worcester
Shrewsbury
Northborough
Southborough
Marlborough
Framingham
Wayland
Weston
Waltham
Watertown
Cambridge
Cambridge

The Henry Knox Trail

To celebrate our nation's birthday in 1926, the states of New York and Massachusetts placed 56 granite monuments with brass plaques along the path traveled by Henry Knox's Train of Artillery 150 years earlier. Do you have a monument in your town? How many of the monuments have you seen?

Ballads

Soldiers often sang ballads while they marched from battle to battle. Some accompanied the singing with pipes (flutes), fiddles (violins), and drums. The singing helped keep the soldiers in good spirits. The beat of the music helped them march in time together. Memorizing the stories kept the soldiers from getting bored.

Ballads help people pass their history from generation to generation. I wrote this ballad for my grandsons, James, Felix, and Chase, to pass on this story about their great-great-great-great-great-great-great-grandfather Major General Henry Knox.

Mary Ames Mitchell
September 2017

More works by this author:
www.MaryAmesMitchell.com

Made in the USA
Middletown, DE
23 July 2019